Cambridge **Discovery Education**™
▶ **INTERACTIVE READERS**

Series editor: Bob Hastings

DEADLY ANIMALS

Kenna Bou...

CAMBRIDGE UNIVERSITY PRESS
Cambridge, New York, Melbourne, Madrid, Cape Town,
Singapore, São Paulo, Delhi, Mexico City

Cambridge University Press
32 Avenue of the Americas, New York, NY 10013-2473, USA

www.cambridge.org
Information on this title: www.cambridge.org/9781107693715

© Cambridge University Press 2014

This publication is in copyright. Subject to statutory exception and to the provisions of relevant collective licensing agreements, no reproduction of any part may take place without the written permission of Cambridge University Press.

First published 2014

Printed in Hong Kong, China, by Golden Cup Printing Company Limited

A catalog record for this publication is available from the British Library.

Library of Congress Cataloging-in-Publication Data

Bourke, Kenna.
 Deadly animals / Kenna Bourke.
   pages cm. -- (Cambridge discovery interactive readers)
 ISBN 978-1-107-69371-5 (pbk. : alk. paper)
 1. Dangerous animals--Juvenile literature. 2. English language--Textbooks for foreign speakers. 3. Readers (Elementary) I. Title.

QL100.B63 2013
591.6'5--dc23
                            2013025119

ISBN 978-1-107-69371-5

Additional resources for this publication at www.cambridge.org

Cambridge University Press has no responsibility for the persistence or accuracy of URLs for external or third-party Internet Web sites referred to in this publication and does not guarantee that any content on such Web sites is, or will remain, accurate or appropriate.

Layout services, art direction, book design, and photo research: Q2ABillSMITH GROUP
Editorial services: Hyphen S.A.
Audio production: CityVox, New York
Video production: Q2ABillSMITH GROUP

Contents

Before You Read: Get Ready! **4**

CHAPTER 1
Watch Out! **6**

CHAPTER 2
Deadly Animals, Big and Small **8**

CHAPTER 3
What Do You Think? **20**

After You Read **22**

Answer Key **24**

Glossary

Before You Read:
Get Ready!

You can die if you meet something deadly. Weather can be deadly. Cars can be deadly. Animals can be really deadly. You can die in only a few minutes because of some deadly animals.

Words to Know

Look at the pictures. Then complete the sentences below with the correct words.

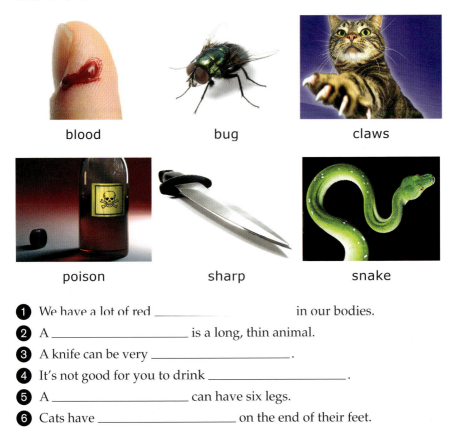

blood   bug   claws

poison   sharp   snake

1. We have a lot of red _____ in our bodies.
2. A _____ is a long, thin animal.
3. A knife can be very _____.
4. It's not good for you to drink _____.
5. A _____ can have six legs.
6. Cats have _____ on the end of their feet.

Words to Know

Read the paragraph. Then complete the sentences below with the correct highlighted words.

There are different kinds of animals. Some are mammals. Mammals give their babies milk to drink. A cow is a mammal, and so is a dog.

A predator is an animal that kills another animal, usually for food. An example of this is a cat killing a bird. The cat is the predator and the bird is the prey. Some animals bite with their teeth. Mosquitoes can bite you, too. Some bugs, like bees, can sting you. Sometimes you get a disease from a bite or sting. A disease makes you feel very sick.

1. A dog can't _____ you, but a bee can!
2. You _____ into an apple when you eat it.
3. Doctors can usually help you with a _____.
4. When a dog eats a rabbit, the dog is the _____, and the rabbit is its _____.
5. Snakes don't give their babies milk. They're not _____.
6. He doesn't like bugs. He _____ them with his foot when he sees them.

Bees

A mosquito

CHAPTER 1

Watch Out!

THE WORLD IS A BIG PLACE. AND OFTEN THE THINGS THAT HAPPEN IN IT AREN'T VERY NICE.

Think about it – every living thing needs food. Many animals and people only eat plants. But other animals and people eat meat. Big animals eat small animals. Small animals usually eat even smaller animals. But some small animals eat big animals.

It's an exciting world, but it isn't safe. Many animals run away from predators all their lives. And when they're not doing that, they're running after their prey.

Animals kill for food, but they also kill to stay **alive**, to stop predators from killing them.

In one way or another, most animals are **deadly**!

ANALYZE
You know that animals sometimes kill people. Why do people kill animals?

What about people? Well, we're really deadly. We eat lots of animals and kill others just for fun.

Most **humans** live in towns and cities. We aren't always looking behind us to see if an animal wants an easy meal. We don't have to run from deadly predators every time we walk down the street.

But some animals kill people. Why do they do that? Is it because they don't like us? Or because we try to kill them? Or is it because they're HUNGRY?

A mosquito uses tubes to drink your blood.

CHAPTER 2

Deadly Animals, Big and Small

THERE ARE MANY DEADLY ANIMALS IN THE WORLD, AND THEY KILL IN MANY DIFFERENT WAYS!

Meet the flying killer: the mosquito! It lives almost everywhere and kills more people than any other animal!

Mosquitoes kill more people every five minutes than sharks kill in a whole year. Over 2.7 million people die every year because of this nasty[1] little bug. But how does it kill? Mosquitoes have diseases like malaria and yellow fever, and those diseases can kill.

Mosquitoes drink your blood. See that mosquito on your arm? It's putting two tubes into you. One tube takes blood; the other stops your blood from getting dry so it can drink more. Delicious![2]

[1] **nasty:** very bad
[2] **delicious:** very good to eat

Feeling hungry? How about some nice fish?

When you go to a restaurant in Japan, ask for puffer fish, or *fugu* in Japanese. Make sure the fugu chef knows what he's doing! This fish is full of poison. One fish can kill 30 people.

If the chef doesn't take out the poison, you can die quickly or you can die slowly. It can take 20 minutes or many hours. The poison goes through your body. First, you can't walk. Next, you can't **breathe**. And then, you're dead.

There are no **medicines** to stop the poison, but sometimes you can stop the poison if you vomit.[3]

[3] **vomit:** when food comes up and out of your mouth

? UNDERSTAND
What are two ways an animal can kill you?

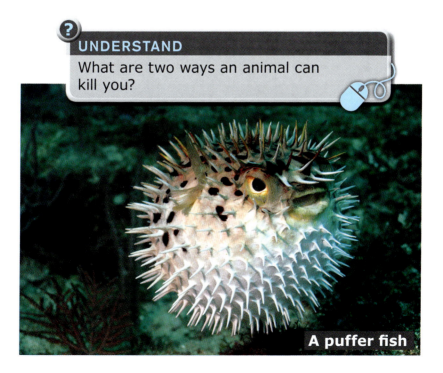

A puffer fish

9

Look at the baby polar bear. Don't you love it?

Now look at the photo above. That's the polar bear just a few years later.

Polar bears have sharp claws and teeth. They swim and run fast, and they're big. They can be 2.5 meters tall, and some weigh as much as 720 kilograms. That's a lot of bear.

A baby polar bear

Polar bears eat birds, fish, and other sea animals. They live in very cold places, like Alaska, so they don't usually see many humans.

But the world is getting warmer. It's harder for bears to find food. So they come nearer to places where people live. Sometimes they're so hungry they kill and eat people. But don't worry! It doesn't happen often.

"I can see you with my 24 eyes!" Yes, that's right. Box jellyfish have 24 eyes – six eyes in four places! But their tentacles are what you need to worry about. Tentacles are the things that look like long legs. There are as many as 60 of them on a box jellyfish. And each one has 5,000 ways to sting you. Oh, and kill you.

You can't see these jellyfish in water. That's a problem. Swim into a box jellyfish by **accident** and the tentacles poison you. You now have only about five minutes to say goodbye to your friends and family. These jellyfish are some of the fastest killers on Earth.

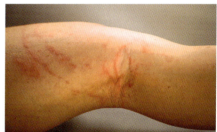

These are jellyfish stings on someone's leg. Not a good vacation!

Video Quest

Shark Attack

Watch the video of a great white shark. Why is it deadly? Why did it bite the man?

11

Let's get out of the water and go and see something cute. Here's the slow loris from the jungles[4] of southeast Asia.

Look at those big brown eyes! It's almost like a toy bear. What a sweet, friendly little animal.

Or is it?

The slow loris does an unusual thing. It keeps poison under its arms. Then it takes the poison, puts it in its mouth, and bites you. Bam! You go into shock. That means it's very difficult for you to breathe, and you need a doctor fast. The shock can kill some people.

[4]**jungle:** a place where it is very hot and there are many trees

This cute slow loris is really not so cute.

Ah, good! Here's an animal that only eats vegetables. It's a hippo. Hippos eat grass and other plants at night. In the day, they're in the water. They look a little funny, too . . . until you get close.

Did you know hippos kill more people than any other mammal in Africa? Hippos are bad-tempered[5] animals. They don't like it when you get close, especially to their babies.

They have long sharp teeth. They're heavy, over 3,000 kilograms! They don't look fast, but they can run 50 kilometers an hour. If a hippo catches you, it isn't funny. It's usually deadly.

[5]**bad-tempered:** get angry very easily

People call the Lonomia caterpillar "the lazy clown" because it looks like a clown and it's slow. Clowns are funny, but these animals can be deadly.

Lonomia caterpillars live on trees in the rainforests[6] of South America. The problem is they're difficult to see. People **touch** them by accident. Also, they live in groups, so you can touch more than one. These caterpillars have 5-centimeter-long **poisonous** spikes. It doesn't **hurt** if you touch a spike, but a day or more later your body starts **bleeding** inside and outside. That hurts! You're in a lot of **pain**. Then, important parts of your body stop working. It's time to see a doctor.

---
[6]**rainforests:** warm places with many trees and where it rains a lot

? ANALYZE
What are some ways that an animal can kill a person by accident?

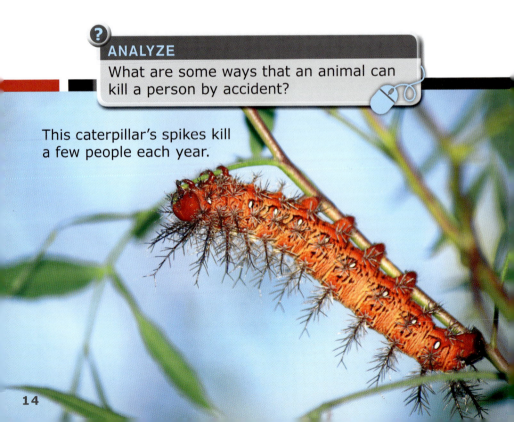

This caterpillar's spikes kill a few people each year.

14

Meet Gustave and his crocodile friends. People say he ate 300 humans, but he's still hungry!

In January 2013, the people from a village in South Africa went into their houses and didn't come out for a long time. Why? Because 15,000 Nile crocodiles ran away from a crocodile farm. And the people knew that crocodiles are deadly.

Nile crocodiles are the biggest crocodiles in Africa – about 3.5 to 5 meters long. And they have more than 60 teeth. That's very good for eating meat. They open their mouths, catch an animal like a small hippo (or maybe a human), and take it underwater where it can't breathe. Then dinner's ready!

Video Quest

Elephant Mother

Watch the video about a mother elephant and her babies. Does she run at the people or leave them alone?

15

The poison dart frog is ten times more poisonous than the puffer fish.

This colorful animal can be red, blue, yellow, black, or green. It's small, about as long as your little finger, and very cute, too. Meet the poison dart frog.

With a name like that, there has to be a problem. Well, yes, it's poisonous. It gets its poison from the bugs it eats. The poison doesn't kill it. The poison stays inside the frog until you touch it. One frog has enough poison to kill ten people. And the doctor can't help.

But it's not all bad. Frog poison, like some snake poisons, is a painkiller. People want to use this poison to make medicines.

Do you remember getting sick, having a toothache, or feeling hungry? It's no fun, is it? Animals get sick and hungry, too, and sometimes that's why they kill people.

In 1898, some workers in Kenya had to build a bridge. For nine months, two African lions called "The Man-eaters of Tsavo" came at night and killed one worker after another. But why?

People think the lions were sick and hungry. A disease in Kenya killed the lions' normal prey. One of the lions also had a bad tooth, so it couldn't catch animals so well. People were easy to catch and eat!

African lions

So there are deadly animals in water and on land. Are there dangerous animals in the sky? Not many. Birds don't usually want to kill people, and that's good for us because some of them probably can!

Let's look at the cassowary, for example. It lives in New Guinea and Australia.

Cassowary facts	
How tall?	2 meters
How heavy?	55–60 kilograms
How fast?	50 kilometers an hour
How many toes?	Three – and one has a 12.5-centimenter-long sharp claw

Do you see the problem? Its big toe is so sharp it can cut your body open. And 50 kilometers an hour is fast. You really don't want a cassowary to run into you!

A cassowary

A cassowary's sharp claws

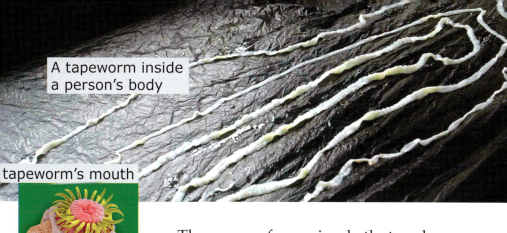

A tapeworm inside a person's body

tapeworm's mouth

There are a few animals that make people go "UGH!" and here's one of them. Think about this. You eat a big meal, but you still feel hungry. For days you eat and eat, but you get thinner and thinner. Why? Because inside your stomach,[7] something is eating the food you eat. Hello, tapeworm!

Tapeworms eat your food, but they can also give you a disease. Maybe you think they're small because they live inside you. But they're not small! Adult tapeworms can be 15 meters long. You get them from eating meat that isn't cooked well. Are you sure you want a hamburger for lunch?

[7] **stomach:** the part inside your body where food goes

Video Quest

King Cobra

Watch this video to find out about the king cobra snake. How long is this one? What do king cobras eat?

19

CHAPTER 3
What Do You Think?

YOU GOT TO THE END OF THE BOOK ALIVE. CONGRATULATIONS!

Read the quiz. What's the right thing to do?

Staying alive			
1. You see a small bear.	Play dead.		Give it some food to eat.	
2. There's a snake in the grass.	Make a SSSSS noise.		Walk away slowly and quietly.	
3. A lion is coming towards you.	Look as big as possible. Put your arms up.		Run really fast and call out for help.	
4. A mosquito is on your leg.	Jump up and down.		Kill it if you can.	
5. There's a hippo running at you.	Shout "STOP" and put one hand up.		Jump to one side.	
6. There is puffer fish on the menu in a restaurant.	Have a hamburger.		Ask for a big one.	

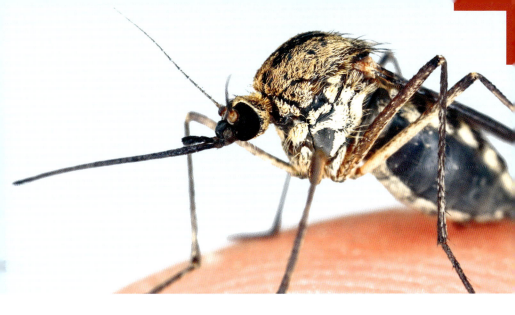

Animals can be deadly. There are cute animals like the big-eyed slow loris; animals that are hard to see like the box jellyfish or the Lonomia caterpillar; and big animals like polar bears, hippos, and crocodiles. They can all kill people. But don't forget, the biggest killer of all is the mosquito!

Most of the animals in this book don't live on your street, but do any live in your country? What's the most dangerous animal you know about?

Answers: 1. Play dead. 2. Walk away slowly and quietly. 3. Look as big as possible. Put your arms up. 4. Kill it if you can. 5. Jump to one side. 6. Have a hamburger.

After You Read

Choose the Correct Answers

Choose Ⓐ, Ⓑ, or Ⓒ to correctly complete the sentences.

❶ There are deadly animals _____.
   Ⓐ in the water
   Ⓑ on land
   Ⓒ in the water and on land

❷ Mosquitoes kill people with _____.
   Ⓐ a disease
   Ⓑ a poison
   Ⓒ their skin

❸ Polar bears live in _____.
   Ⓐ rainforests
   Ⓑ cold places
   Ⓒ warm places

❹ The slow loris keeps poison under _____.
   Ⓐ its ears
   Ⓑ its arms
   Ⓒ its eyes

❺ Hippos eat _____.
   Ⓐ plants
   Ⓑ people
   Ⓒ crocodiles

❻ Poison dart frogs are _____.
   Ⓐ very large
   Ⓑ very friendly
   Ⓒ very small

❼ Cassowaries ae _____.
   Ⓐ mammals
   Ⓑ snakes
   Ⓒ birds

8 Tapeworms make you _____ .
- Ⓐ tired
- Ⓑ thin
- Ⓒ fat

The Deadliest of the Deadly

Write down the three animals from the book that you think are the worst. Why are they worse than the others?

Animal	Why it's so bad

Complete the Text

Use the words in the box to complete the paragraph.

| bite | bugs | diseases | kills | predator | prey | sting |

A **❶** _____ is an animal that **❷** _____ another animal. Small animals, like frogs, are often **❸** _____ for a snake. But how do animals kill? Animals like lions **❹** _____ with their teeth. **❺** _____ like bees can **❻** _____ . There are many kinds of **❼** _____ you can get from animals, and some are deadly.

23

Answer Key

Words to Know, page 4
1 blood **2** snake **3** sharp **4** poison **5** bug **6** claws

Words to Know, page 5
1 sting **2** bite **3** disease **4** predator, prey
5 mammals **6** kills

Analyze, page 7 *Answers will vary.*

Understand, page 9
Some can give you a disease. Others can poison you if you eat them.

Video Quest, page 11
They are big and have sharp teeth. This shark bit the man because it didn't know who or what he was, not to eat him.

Analyze, page 14 *Answers will vary.*

Video Quest, page 15
They think she might charge them, but she doesn't.

Video Quest, page 19
It's three meters long. It eats other snakes.

Choose the Correct Answers, pages 22-23
1 C **2** A **3** B **4** B **5** A **6** C **7** C **8** B

The Deadliest of the Deadly, page 23
Answers will vary.

Complete the Text, page 23
1 predator **2** kills **3** prey **4** bite **5** Bugs **6** sting
7 diseases